FAMILY BUSINESS:
PRACTICAL LEADERSHIP SUCCESSION PLANNING

Exceed Your Expectations

Ronald P. Smyser

abbott press®
A DIVISION OF WRITER'S DIGEST

Copyright © 2013 Ronald P. Smyser.

All rights reserved. No part of this book may be used or reproduced by any means, graphic, electronic, or mechanical, including photocopying, recording, taping or by any information storage retrieval system without the written permission of the publisher except in the case of brief quotations embodied in critical articles and reviews.

Abbott Press books may be ordered through booksellers or by contacting:

Abbott Press
1663 Liberty Drive
Bloomington, IN 47403
www.abbottpress.com
Phone: 1-866-697-5310

Because of the dynamic nature of the Internet, any web addresses or links contained in this book may have changed since publication and may no longer be valid. The views expressed in this work are solely those of the author and do not necessarily reflect the views of the publisher, and the publisher hereby disclaims any responsibility for them.

ISBN: 978-1-4582-1320-4 (sc)
ISBN: 978-1-4582-1319-8 (hc)
ISBN: 978-1-4582-1318-1 (e)

Library of Congress Control Number: 2013922550

Printed in the United States of America.

Abbott Press rev. date: 8/29/2014

To Dianna

Your Values and enduring, affective guidance

are my compass and beacon.

Contents

Introduction ix

Chapter 1	Succession Planning: Why, What, and When 1
Chapter 2	The Benefits of Practical Leadership Succession Planning 17
Chapter 3	What Do Successful Businesses Have in Common? 20
Chapter 4	Does Your Business Have a Future? 24
Chapter 5	Business Survival: Generational Succession Challenges 27
Chapter 6	Leadership Succession Failures: Fifteen Key Causes and Solutions 36
Chapter 7	Effective Delegation: An Exciting Leadership Succession Tool 59

Chapter 8	Job Descriptions: A Key Step to Leadership Success and Practical Leadership Succession	70
Chapter 9	Selecting Leadership Successors; Practical Steps	81
Chapter 10	Helping Your Children Find Their Professional Passions	94
Chapter 11	Creating Commitment and Motivation in a Performance-Oriented Culture	98
Chapter 12	Compensation and Incentives for Success	109
Chapter 13	Practical Leadership Succession Planning: Takeaways	116

Introduction

Congratulations!

Your interest in leadership succession indicates that you are starting a business and planning ahead smartly or, equally exciting, you have created a successful business and want to ensure its future.

If you have already started your business you know that creating, growing and protecting a successful business requires passionate and tireless commitment. Only you will ever fully understand the reasons for the personal sacrifices you've made, for which you may have felt more than occasional skepticism and criticism from others.

The hostile impact of ever-expanding competitive threats; burdensome federal, state and local regulations and taxes; harsh economic conditions; entitlement-driven employees; family business dynamics; and uncontrollable events can at times lead you to question the wisdom of owning a family business.

But nurturing a small business to success is a **very** special accomplishment.

And how wonderfully sweet it is when the business works well!

You know the significance of what you have accomplished and what you are doing for your family, for your community, and for your country.

It has been fallaciously stated recently that you did not build your business, the government did. Those who have never had a real job in which they actually had challenging responsibilities for which they were held accountable, and those who have never created a new business in which they were responsible for the success of the business and the livelihood of their employees might actually believe this banal, self-serving, anti-business, bureaucratic nonsense.

But you know better. ***You are a special breed. You are an Entrepreneur. You have built it!***

Thank you for purchasing **Family Business: Practical Leadership Succession Planning**.

If you seek philosophical discussion, theoretical conjecture, speculation, distracting escape from reality, or unwarranted personal strokes, stop now—you have selected the wrong book.

If you want unvarnished, experience-based assistance—with a focus on how to prevent or resolve leadership succession derailers and set a logical path forward—you've made a great choice; read on.

Leadership succession may appear to be an ominous challenge, but it's not as difficult, mysterious, or complicated as you may have been led to believe.

First, a little background about Spinnaker Leadership Associates, Inc. may be helpful to you.

For more than twenty years we have committed to being an unusually insightful and incisive leadership and business management resource. We are grateful to our clients for seeking our counsel and for allowing us to meet that commitment.

We have been in your shoes, with our own businesses and with our clients' businesses. We understand the extreme difficulty, isolation and pain of leading a family business and the leadership commitment, motivation, patience, and stamina needed to succeed.

Our **Vision**, for our clients and ourselves, is **Preeminent Business Leadership**. We accomplish our **Vision** by offering forthright, insightful leadership and business counsel based exclusively on proven, practical principles. Clients often tell us we succeed in accomplishing that **Vision**.

Our **Values**—the foundation of our commitment, motivation and behavior—include **Integrity, Client Priority, Visionary Anticipation, Leadership, Commitment, Excellence, Precision, Common Sense and Accountability.**

Our focus includes **Individual and Team Leadership Commitment, Motivation and Impact; Leadership Succession Planning; Ownership Succession Planning; Strategic Business Management; Corporate Structuring; and Asset Protection and Preservation.**

Our guidance reflects insights gained from an unrelenting pursuit and implementation of innovative, practical, proven solutions to leadership and business management challenges. Our logical, straightforward recommendations are based on personal and client experiences and on creative, refreshingly practical approaches to otherwise confusing business challenges.

Our clients have included a wide variety of family businesses, privately held businesses, public companies—from recent IPOs to global conglomerates—and nonprofit organizations.

Family Business: Practical Leadership Succession Planning is the first of two books about family business succession. Innovative approaches for practical and effective ownership succession are discussed in our forthcoming book, ***Family Business: Practical Ownership Succession Planning***.

Family Business: Practical Leadership Succession Planning is addressed to those who believe that they have a family business and believe that their children will succeed them. But let's think about that more broadly, because you want your business to continue to grow and prosper. The second-generation leadership could be your children, but, for reasons discussed in this book, there may be better options for the future success of your business. And your children may thank you for considering those alternative options.

To exceed your leadership succession planning expectations, consider the following while reading this book:

1. Use well-founded business leadership principles rather than parental compassion or guilt to guide you.
2. Think like someone who just bought your family business and how that someone would take your business forward. This will help you to be more objective about your leadership succession options and actions.
3. Be realistic about the state of your business enterprise. For example, is it a family business yet or is it your business? Is the business financially successful or marginal? Are prospective successors available or as yet unidentified? What current or future leadership strengths are needed to ensure future success? What leadership vulnerabilities need to be eliminated or overcome?
4. Readily admit any succession mistakes made thus far and, beginning now, personally direct the leadership succession planning and implementation for your business.
5. Identify and eradicate all barriers to leadership succession as though the success and future of your business depend on it—because they do.

6. Consider all options and resources for identifying your successor, no matter what the potential cost might be in social or familial relationships. Give priority to implementing preferred options while planning for and containing the fallout.

7. Consider the examples used throughout this book and their parallels to your business. These examples are real case experiences modified only to protect client confidentiality and provide you with foresight against reinventing the wheel.

8. Take notes as you read, and use the information wisely.

Now, get serious about leadership succession planning, and make it happen. You will be glad that you did.

If at any time you have questions, concerns, or suggestions, please visit our website (www.spinnakerleadership.com) and contact us. We would be delighted to hear from you and would be pleased to assist you.

Sincerely,

Ron Smyser

Founder and Chairman, Spinnaker Leadership Associates, Inc.

Chapter 1

Succession Planning: Why, What, and When

Why do you need succession planning?

If the future financial needs of you or your family are securely met without income from your family business, or if the value and fate of your business after you have left the business, retired, or died are not important to you, leadership succession may not be of interest to you. But keep reading anyway because important information in this book can help you to enhance your leadership impact and make your leadership task easier.

If your family's financial needs depend on the future health and continuity of your business, or if the future of your business is in any other way important to you, a practical and effective succession plan must be put in place as soon as possible. Read on.

What is succession planning?

Succession planning is essential to the continuing success and the future of your business. Succession planning must not be delegated to your advisors or subordinates. It is one of the most important things you should do as the leader of your business.

You created and built your business. Now, with the same passion and commitment that made your business successful, focus on (1) leading its continuing success through your generation and future generations (family or nonfamily) or (2) defining alternatives—for example, selling the business—that capture the full value of the family enterprise for you and your family.

There are two separate but interacting parts of succession planning—leadership succession planning and ownership succession planning.

Leadership succession planning is the process of identifying, evaluating, selecting, mentoring, and motivating your replacement. For your business to continue successfully, it must have at least the same level of future leadership capability and commitment that made it successful in the first place.

Where would your business be if you had not had both the capability and commitment to create and build it? Where **will** your business be if your strengths, your special talents, your commitment and your leadership are not sufficiently replaced and continued?

The new leadership must be as good as or better than you have been at doing your job. It may be true that the new leadership will "inherit" a successful business, while you had the more difficult task of creating one. But the ongoing challenges to the business are ever-increasingly more ominous and complex than they were when you started the business. Therefore, your successor must be thoroughly qualified, prepared and motivated for his or her new assignment.

Ownership succession planning is the second part of succession planning and is the process of creating a preferred path to transfer control of the business from you to someone else. Well-prepared and implemented ownership succession planning (1) can help motivate future leaders of the business, (2) dictates how control of the business will pass through generations, and (3) has value in that it can help protect an estate from unnecessary tax issues after the owner is gone.

Often when lawyers, accountants and financial advisors refer to succession planning, their focus is on **ownership** succession. Therefore, their advice centers primarily on protecting your estate from taxes and other threats, *after you're gone*. Some advisors actually call succession "the final act."

Advisors often take for granted that a leadership succession will somehow take place. And they may believe that they are more qualified than you are to select your successor.

Advisors may propose that a trust fund will stipulate the terms and conditions of leadership succession and ownership succession (terrible idea). They may even plan to participate in the succession implementation after you are gone (even worse idea).

Ownership succession planning without prior practical and effective leadership succession planning places the cart before the horse. Without a clear, effective leadership succession plan in place, ownership succession may be just passing to the next generation (your children or others) a hollow shell that will implode in the near future.

Consider this example:

A founder of a successful family business unexpectedly died at the age of sixty-nine. His wife and four grown children were understandably devastated.

Upon their dad's death, the children (employees) were surprised to learn for the first time that, during prior "succession planning," the company ownership had been transferred to a trust fund. The trust fund stipulated that, upon the death of the founder, his wife would become the business leader, and upon her death, the company ownership would transfer in equal parts to the grown children. This approach and the structure of the Board of Directors ultimately placed the legal advisor in charge of implementing the details of the succession plan.

The founder's wife was financially secure—as long as the business continued successfully. But unfortunately, as is often the case with family businesses, the business was now in deep trouble.

At the age of sixty-nine the founder had continued to be closely involved in and personally directed every activity of the business. When suddenly he was gone, the visionary, the rainmaker, the sales and marketing strategist, the networker, the hour-to-hour, day-to-day operations leader, and the financier—all of them—were suddenly gone.

Since the founder's wife had not been deeply involved in running the business before her husband died, she was unprepared to lead the business after he left. No one had a good grasp of specifically what the founder had been doing or precisely how he did it, so no one was prepared to seamlessly and effectively carry out his responsibilities. Equally troublesome, the four siblings were unsure about their authority and respective business responsibilities and in conflict about who should now lead the company.

Pandemonium set in at the company. Leadership deteriorated. Sales quotations went without effective follow-up. Local networking, a major source of new business, all but ceased. The competitive position eroded. Fearful of the company's future, key employees left for other job opportunities.

Siblings struggled with their individual responsibilities, authority levels, career aspirations, and self-centered interest in how the stipulations of the trust fund could be selectively beneficial.

Within eighteen months, revenues had declined by more than 50 percent, and the estimated net value (assets minus liabilities) of the family enterprise had decreased by more than 70 percent.

Sometime in the future this business will be further rocked by the trust fund stipulation for equal split of future ownership—control of the business. Equally split ownership can create control chaos.

The succession plan for this business failed to provide continuity of leadership for the business and set the business on a course of failure.

Unless an effective, practical leadership succession plan is created and implemented quickly, followed by development and implementation of a practical ownership succession plan that corrects the mistakes made thus far—before the founder's wife departs or becomes incapacitated—this business will most likely fail in the early years of second-generation leadership.

Leadership succession planning cannot prevent the personal tragedy of a sudden death of the family business founder and leader, but it can help ensure financial security for the family and continuity of the business through generations.

If ownership succession implementation takes place or is dictated before there is sufficient progress with leadership succession planning, the leadership succession may be ineffective. In that event, a negative outcome for the future of the business is often predictable.

Equally split ownership for the next generation is an emotionally driven parental impulse based primarily on the need to treat all children equally or to not show favoritism. And it is often encouraged by business advisors who have insufficient family business experience to know better or the courage to push back on the idea for fear of losing the account.

Equally split ownership derails future leadership success, defies sound business logic and should be avoided. Why would the most capable potential leaders of the next generation step up to the leadership bar when their counterparts can easily veto their plans? Why would nonfamily members want to lead your business if your children have parochially based, individual objectives and cumulative overriding control positions?

When you started your business would you have put yourself in the situation of being susceptible to someone else outvoting you? Don't do it to your potential successor. Alternative, viable ownership control succession options (discussed in our forthcoming book) can provide sufficient autonomy to new leaders while preserving and protecting the assets of the family enterprise.

Focus first on leadership succession planning. Then, rather than using equally split ownership or some other such ineffective advisor fad, structure ownership succession to support your successor who will have full responsibility to lead once your departure takes place. If you cannot do this because you have not yet chosen your successor, stop procrastinating and prepare your leadership succession plan. If for any reason you believe that you cannot provide future ownership support to your chosen successor, then (it seems obvious) you have not chosen the right successor.

When should you start succession planning?

When you start the business and create your formal business structure is an ideal time to start your succession planning. If not then, as soon as possible would be a good time. It is never too soon to start your succession planning. The alternative—starting too late—can be disastrous.

If you have children, and you wait until your retirement to implement leadership succession, your kids will probably not have waited to step in and lead the business. And unless you have forced them to stay, the most qualified of your children will have already created their own professional careers elsewhere.

If you wait until your will is being read to identity your successor, you may have avoided this important (and often mistakenly dreaded) part of your leadership responsibility — communicating the new leader and leadership structure to your family. But how well will it work for the future of your business and your family?

You help raise your children while you are also busy growing the business. Doesn't it make sense—when they are ready—to ask them if they want to help you grow the business or to initiate better, alternative practical leadership succession plans, while you are still active in and available to the business?

Why aren't family business founders more successful in implementing leadership succession?

First, it is the odd entrepreneurial duck that wants to plan his or her replacement, especially when there are no plans to retire or die anytime soon.

Second, to most family business founders the whole "leadership succession thing" appears to be an undecipherable, complicated challenge that offers only an emotional headache in choosing between siblings. And the path to succession seems to be difficult and lonely.

Third, it often seems less stressful to just put off leadership succession planning (like putting off funeral arrangements) in favor of other priorities. So, that is what happens … until it is too late. Meanwhile, implied or direct promises of ownership are often made to the second generation, creating a birthright entitlement and/or an obligation to work in the family business.

Should co-leader positions be established when there are multiple prospective future leaders, for example two sons?

A terrible idea. But it seems to pop up when a compassionate parent is trying to avoid a tough business decision (appointing a successor) or wants to replace him or herself with dual not-yet-ready-for-prime-time leadership candidates.

Think about it. Does the business now require two leaders, when it needed only one previously? If you were hiring your replacement from the outside world, would you seek (and pay for) co-leaders? If so, would your two sons be the most qualified candidates from the world's supply of leadership candidates? Did you say yes? Really?

How well would co-leadership have worked out for you when you created and developed the business?

Also, once again think like someone who has just bought your business. He or she would put the priorities and needs of the business well above the needs of the former owner's family. The number and types of jobs that the business requires would be determined. The qualifications and requirements of each job and the qualifications and performance of each potential job candidate would be defined before the leadership team was identified and confirmed.

Co-leadership may sound good, but singular, focused leadership is more likely to be the best path forward.

The priorities and needs of the business, not the number of available family members nor the needs of family members, determine the number and types of leadership and other positions required.

How will you know when the leadership succession implementation plan is being successful?

Leadership succession planning and implementation is an ongoing process. When you work directly with your second generation and others in a confidential but open, forthright approach to develop a leadership succession plan, you can build credibility for the process and encourage creativity and cohesiveness to support the outcome.

Along the way, progress in leadership succession planning becomes self-evident as the plan is developed and implemented.

For example, if your successor will replace your strengths and special talents and perform as well as or better than you have performed on your key leadership responsibilities and functions, you're off to a good start.

If the prospective leaders understand and are committed to their future roles and responsibilities, your leadership succession plan is on track.

If they also know and respect the sequence of and the participants in replacing your strengths, talents, and functions, your leadership succession plan is progressing well.

If your leadership succession is planned and implemented well, your confidence in the plan and your successor will, over time, enable you to diminish your direct leadership role. Soon after you have begun to release some of your official roles and responsibilities, you will start to feel the freedom to choose how much or how little you want to participate in the ongoing leadership of the business and can focus on strategic rather than tactical challenges—another sign of good progress.

Summary:

If you want your business to continue to prosper now and into and through the second generation, you should implement a well-considered and well-executed leadership succession plan as soon as possible.

By wisely developing and objectively choosing your successor well before you plan to exit the business, you give your business a much better chance to (1) continue to prosper through your generation, (2) support you in your current and future alternative adventures, and (3) survive through the second generation.

Subsequently, you should start to create a common-sense ownership succession plan that supports your successor, enables your successor to lead without unnecessary interference, fosters cooperation among current and future family members, preserves and protects family enterprise assets, and enables you to maintain control as long as is necessary.

Unfortunately, entrenched advisors, who have not been in your shoes or have not kept up with what works well, often offer succession advice that may be off target or totally misleading.

But, fortunately, creative, practical leadership and ownership succession tools are now available for you to accomplish the above objectives.

So, procrastinate no longer. Give succession the same level of unbiased attention, objectivity, and planning that you would give to any serious threat to your family enterprise and ... get on with it.

Chapter 2

The Benefits of Practical Leadership Succession Planning

A practical and effective leadership succession plan provides the following important benefits:

1. Helps identify and confirm the most qualified leadership successor candidates and appropriate leadership succession structuring.
2. Fosters continuing success of the business through the first and successive generations.
3. Informs family or second-generation members about specifically what needs to be done and who should do it ... in the unlikely event that something happens to you.
4. Encourages members of the second generation to work together to successfully create and implement a seamless leadership progression and succession.

5. Shows each member of the second generation how best to use his or her talents for the business and/or individual career success.
6. Assists each member of the second generation to (1) realize that not everyone should or will achieve the top leadership position and (2) endorse leadership appointments that support and grow the business.
7. Ensures that successful ongoing leadership is in place while you are available to facilitate leadership succession—before you inadvertently or purposely release control to the second generation.
8. Promotes leadership commitment and motivation in the second generation through performance-based compensation and incentives, *not* entitlements.
9. Provides opportunities for you to assist members of the second generation with new challenges from their respective increasing professional responsibilities within or outside of your business.
10. Helps you to focus on strategic business activities (visionary planning, rainmaking, networking for the business and community involvement) rather than tactical activities, as you also move more to other

adventures (golf, sailing, parachute jumping, painting, clipping coupons, counting your money, etc.).

11. Enhances your leadership impact, efficiency, and rewards.
12. Creates a foundation and identifies preferred decision options for logical, practical, and effective ownership succession.
13. Helps ensure ever-increasing financial wealth for the first and each successive generation.

Chapter 3

What Do Successful Businesses Have in Common?

"Visionary companies are premier institutions—the crown jewels—in their industries, widely admired by their peers and having a long track record of making a significant impact on the world around them."

—Jim Collins and Jerry Porras

In chapter 1 of **Built to Last**, Jim Collins and Jerry Porras provided significant information about what they called Visionary (more than successful) companies and listed the following common characteristics:

- ❖ Premier institution in its industry
- ❖ Widely admired by knowledgeable business people
- ❖ Made an indelible imprint on the world in which we live
- ❖ Had multiple generations of chief executives

❖ Been through multiple product (or service) life cycles

❖ Founded before 1950

Built to Last also discussed the habits of Visionary companies—American Express, Boeing, Ford, General Electric, Hewlett-Packard, IBM, Johnson & Johnson, Marriott, Motorola, Nordstrom, Proctor & Gamble, Sony, Wal-Mart, and Walt Disney and comparison companies.

You might be wondering how habits of the big companies relate to your business. Remember that almost all companies were once small start-ups, often founded, launched, and grown to success by friends or family members. When **Built to Last** was written, the above-named companies were beyond three generations. Obviously, they were doing many things right. The elements of the success of small companies that grow through generations into big companies can be informative.

But, less than 50 percent of small businesses succeed to the second generation. And, less than 15 percent of small businesses succeed to the third generation.

Consider the behaviors of successful family businesses. In our experience, the most successful privately held or family businesses, from startups to family owned global conglomerates, demonstrate many or most of the following key behavioral guiding principles:

- Clear, articulated, and implemented Vision, Values, Priorities, and Strategies
- An unrelenting drive to be the "Best of the Best"
- A written business plan that creates focus for key priorities, strategies, and actions
- Talented, effective leaders and others throughout the organization who (1) lead by example, (2) delegate well, (3) are customer centric, (4) are bottom-line focused, (5) have impact beyond their own responsibilities, (6) plan and communicate well, and (7) listen … listen … learn … lead
- A demonstrated, consistent, tenacious drive to anticipate and meet customer priorities and needs
- Creation and continuous fostering of commitment and motivation in a performance-oriented culture
- Selective employment, placement, challenge, and development of qualified candidates for each and every job in the business
- Clarity of responsibilities and accountability for results
- Focused net cash flow management

- ❖ The creation and preservation of substantial cash reserves for operating, growing, and protecting the business
- ❖ A well-conceived leadership development and succession plan that is implemented at all levels of the organization

How does your business stack up to the above list?

What should you do differently, starting now? Read on.

Chapter 4

Does Your Business Have a Future?

If you have started your business recently, and your need for second-generation participation is not imminent, what you have is *your* business, but it is not yet a *family business*. As you move forward, give serious consideration to the suggestions in this book.

If you already have or anticipate second-generation participation and if you were totally objective, how would you describe the state of your family business? Let's keep it simple. Pick one of the following three options:

1. A Family Business with a Future:

    Currently employed or to-be-employed members of the next generation (including children, extended family members, nonfamily employees, and others) fully understand the

Vision, Mission, Values, Strategies, and Priorities of the business. They are committed, productive participants who set an example for others and strive to grow, preserve, and protect the business. They and the business live within or below their true earning potential. Founders, shareholders, leaders, and employees have confidence in the team and the future of the business.

2. Grim Reaper Bait:

Employed members of the next generation (family or others) are occasionally productive participants, sometimes set an example but often watch things happen, and are frequently paid more than they can earn elsewhere. Founders struggle with business growth, bottom line results, and consistent cash flow.

3. Dead Business Walking:

Members of the next generation (family or others) are employed by the business while they pursue other professional aspirations, often look to be led, frequently don't know what's happening, and are paid above their true earning capability. The business struggles with more than occasional negative cash flow as it subsidizes the family's growing needs.

Unfortunately, too many family businesses are best described by option No. 2 or No. 3.

If you picked option No. 1, lucky you. You are either in la-la land and life is still good, or you have succeeded against significant odds. In either case, you have a lot to gain from a well-planned and implemented, practical leadership succession plan.

If you picked option No. 2, it's not yet too late. You must make some important changes in culture and personnel to turn the ship around. And you have a great deal to gain from a well-planned and implemented, practical leadership succession plan.

If you picked option No. 3, try to find someone out there who will take this thing off your hands before its value turns negative— or consider shutting the business down before it consumes more of your resources. But first, read on. Maybe some quick counter measures can still save your business.

Chapter 5

Business Survival: Generational Succession Challenges

"Would anyone say the best way to pick a championship Olympic team is to select the sons and daughters of those who won 20 years ago? Giving someone a favored position just because his old man accomplished something would be a crazy way for a society to compete."

—Warren Buffett

Less than 15 percent of family businesses succeed into and through the second generation. If you believe your business will be in the successful 15 percent, you are not alone. Others feel the same way about their businesses. But keep in mind that, from the time that the leadership begins moving to the second generation, there is an 85 percent probability of business failure.

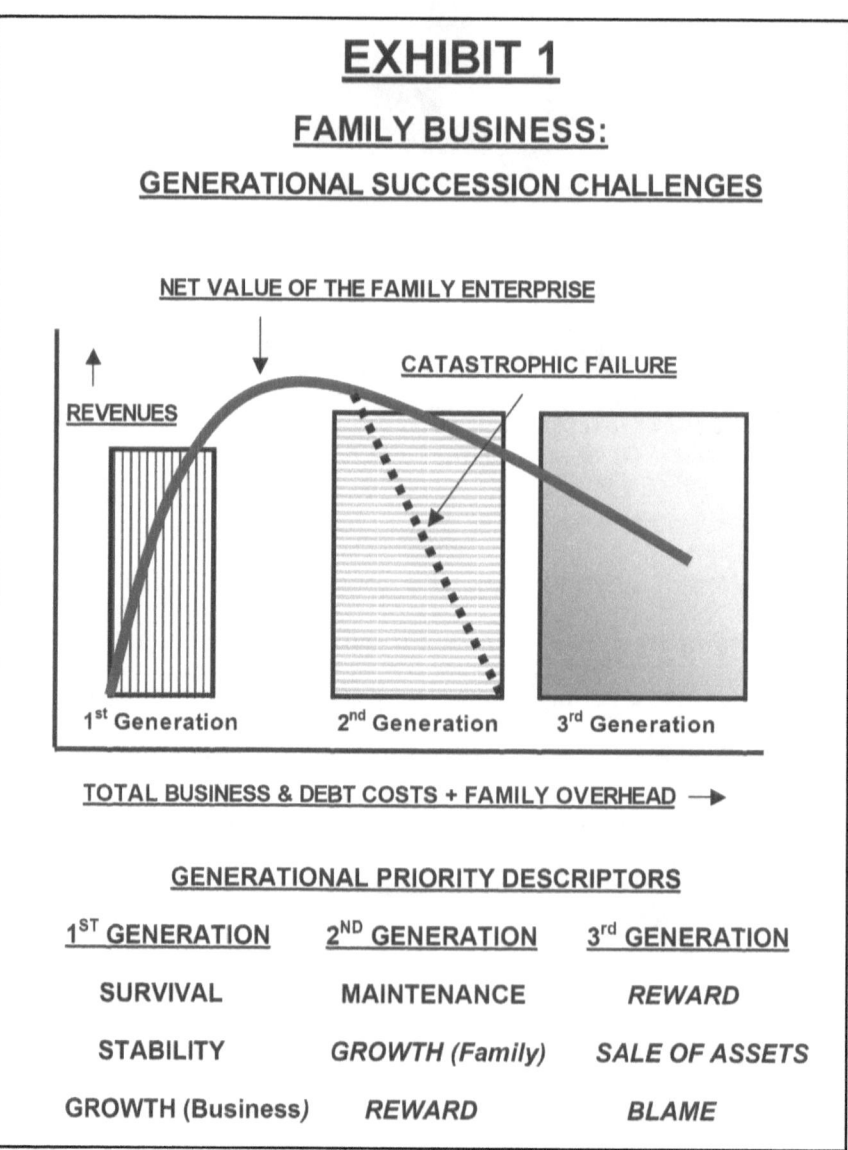

Exhibit 1, "Family Business: Generational Succession Challenges," is a graphical depiction of the financial progress through three generations of an initially successful family business.

Revenues are shown on the vertical axis. The total of business operating and debt costs plus family lifestyle overhead costs are shown on the horizontal axis. The Net Value of the Family Enterprise (Essentially, the value of the family enterprise assets minus liabilities; see Exhibit 2) is represented by the black curve. Potential catastrophic failure of the business is represented by the dashed line.

In Exhibit 1, the most common leadership priorities of each of the three generations are shown as Generational Priority Descriptors.

The Generational Priority Descriptors during the first generation of a business are often Survival, Stability, and Growth of the business. The Generational Priority Descriptors during the second generation are often Maintenance, Growth of the family, and Reward. The Generational Priority Descriptors during the third generation are often Reward, Sale of Assets, and Blame.

In the first generation of a family business mom and pop create and lead the business while they live a modest lifestyle. Their leadership priorities are typically based on survival, financial stability, and growth of the business. They take only modest compensation and put most of the annual net proceeds back into the business for future growth and accumulation of cash reserves.

During the first generation, revenues grow while family overhead, operating costs, and debt levels grow also, but at a carefully controlled rate. Annual net cash flow increases nicely as revenues increase. The net value of the family enterprise increases impressively during this first generation of a successful business.

As the second generation gets involved in leading the business—even at low to middle management levels—the story almost always (85 percent chance) changes dramatically.

Second-generation leadership priorities are often based on maintenance of the original business, taking care of growing families, and reward–creating personal lifestyles that are better than the lifestyle of their parents. As will be discussed later, professional passions of the second generation almost always differ from the professional passions of the business founder. Consequently, members of the second generation are not as committed to or motivated by the existing business, **a business that was not created by them**. Members of this generation often seek to diversify the business to create something that can provide them with their own identify.

During second-generation leadership, revenues grow, but business operating costs, business debt-level costs and family overhead (mouths to feed, lifestyles, etc.) costs increase at a significantly faster rate. Annual net free cash flow diminishes, and cash reserves flatten or decrease. The net value of the family enterprise declines.

During this period, the business becomes increasingly vulnerable to (1) the changing interests of its leadership, (2) disruptive internal dynamics, (3) diminishing competitive capability, and (4) decline of cash reserves. If unanticipated threats—for example, deteriorating economic conditions or new competitive threats—merge with the increasing vulnerabilities of the business and create a cumulative challenge that the business cannot overcome, the business can fail catastrophically.

When the third generation gets involved in the business (if the business reaches this generation) the trend to better lifestyles and the interest in diversifying to other business areas escalate. Revenues during this period often stay essentially flat or decline while the business and debt-level costs plus family lifestyle costs grow rapidly. The same business vulnerabilities as described above increase, and the weakened business is even more susceptible to unanticipated threats. The business and family cash needs can quickly overcome the capability of the family business to produce sufficient cash flow.

Members of the third generation often sell off family business assets to maintain their lifestyles for as long as possible, while they blame other things—such as their ancestors, siblings, competition and the economic environment—for the demise of the "golden goose."

The above-outlined generational priority characteristics during the second and third generations are primary causes of the failure of family businesses.

Exhibit 2

Family Business: Net Value of the Family Enterprise

1. Owner net cash flow, compensation, perks, and benefits

2. Cash reserves and other assets minus liabilities

3. Revenues, trend, and stability

4. Gross margin

5. Preservation and growth of net assets

6. Financial stability

7. Market share position, trend, and stability

8. Competitive position and capabilities

9. Industry and geographical position

10. Brand identification and prestige

11. Leadership breadth, depth, network, and succession capability

12. Growth trends

13. Growth and development of employees and future generations

14. Employment level, resources, and trends

15. Community recognition and impact

16. Philanthropy

Where is your business on the "Net Value of the Enterprise" curve? A quick check of the trend in the last five years of your owner's net cash flow, cash reserves and other assets minus liabilities, revenues, gross margin, market share position, and competitive position, can provide valuable insight. What actions seem appropriate?

Summary:

> If you want your business to survive during the first generation and to and through the second generation, (1) focus on continually driving the net value of the family enterprise skyward and (2) pay special attention to anticipating, identifying, and avoiding or correcting generational leadership priority behaviors that can threaten the family business.

The stakes are high. But the work is not difficult. It takes focus, discipline, common sense, and an informed, practical leadership succession plan.

Key causes of and suggested solutions for generational leadership priority issues are discussed in chapter 6.

Chapter 6

Leadership Succession Failures: Fifteen Key Causes and Solutions

"People are your most important asset turns out to be wrong. People are not your most important asset. The right people are."

—Jim Collins

When leadership behavioral priorities (chapter 5, Exhibit 1) shift from Survival, Stability and Business Growth to Maintenance, Family Growth and Reward, the Net Value of the Family Enterprise levels or declines and business failure is predictable. Often, these events closely correspond with increasing involvement of successive generations in middle to upper leadership positions.

Causes of the shift in leadership behavioral priorities and subsequent business failure—and suggested solutions—are outlined below in an approximately descending order of impact on the business. These causes of business failure should be given high priority for appropriate corrective actions with a strong sense of urgency.

1. Entitlements:

An entitlement culture often emerges and expands as a business, particularly a family business with second-generation participation, becomes successful. Call it "success breeds failure." Entitlements come in many shapes and sizes and, like cancer, enter all aspects of a business, attacking the health of the host.

Family members of the second generation have usually experienced more personal income and entitlements than did their parents. They may also be receiving guaranteed income from family trust funds (a really bad idea, no matter the reason for doing it). Therefore, members of the second generation naturally become more interested in living "the good life" and less motivated than their parents were to personally commit to lead, preserve, and protect the business *that they did not create*. They tend to take more out of the business each year because their lifestyle level requires it, and they may believe that they deserve it.

If the above description fits your business, take steps immediately to rectify the situation or think seriously about (1) leadership succession options (chapter 9) other than appointing your children to lead your business in the future, or (2) selling the business in the near future before its marketable net value decreases significantly.

To resolve entitlement issues, lead by example. Require positive commitment, responsible behavior and high productivity and accountability from all employees, especially family members. Regardless of the success level of your business, restrict entitlements that you or your family members take directly as productive employees in the business. *As you did, members of the next generation must earn their way or they won't feel the pride of ownership, nor will they properly value the business!*

Often several offspring working in a family business receive the same level of wage or salary compensation regardless of their level of responsibility (as a birthright entitlement). They're paid "what they need" or the same amount that their siblings get, regardless of what the position they hold would pay someone else. This practice may be understandable parental compassion, but it is totally misplaced in and damaging to the business. How would a new, unrelated owner pay for the value received from each of them? Implement accordingly.

Wage or salary employment compensation for you and your family member employees should be determined according to established employment policies (see chapters 8, 11, and 12). For those who are or become shareholders as well as employees, additional income opportunities can be available in the form of shareholder dividends or distributions—when the business is doing well. For those who are not employed by the business or are shareholders only, there is no employee compensation.

As discussed in chapter 12, if your adult children work for your business, they should be treated like all other employees except that they should provide more to the business for less wage or salary compensation. Birthright should be the right to respect and preserve the health of the business, not the right to a special ride at the cost of the business or its other employees.

Employment of your family members should not be an automatic given any more than it is for any other employee. Family members should be required by family business policy to earn their employment opportunity—as the most qualified candidates for jobs at any level. Or they should be required to take employment elsewhere until such time as they can compete as the most qualified candidates for jobs in your business, even when their last name is not on their resume. This policy helps ensure that your children learn what is required to enable the lifestyle they want, how other businesses are run, and how other leaders lead—good or bad. And by sampling other occupations, your children can better define their professional passions and preferred career paths before they or you cement their future in your business.

Children of the founder are often told, or surmise, that they will become owners of the business, and consequently, even when they are not yet shareholders, they may act as privileged shareholders in their relationships with customers, other employees, and suppliers. This behavior encourages family member entitlements and negatively affects customer service and employee morale, and should be detected and eradicated.

If ownership may be in their future, your children should be told well in advance that possible ownership is not a birthright but birthright is an opportunity to earn their position, put their own skin in the game, and be rewarded accordingly. They must earn their position in the business, and they should earn or pay for their opportunity of ownership, if they want to be shareholders of a healthy, growing business.

As the (Eagles) song says, …"**You want to live like a king but the world doesn't owe you a thing. Get over it, get over it".** Seems like a timely message for members of the second generation.

If your adult-age children have been taught to earn their way, congratulations, you have given them an important value. Assuming that they have applicable talents, experiences, and aspirations, they can probably continue to be considered as candidates to succeed you, *if that is what you and what they want.*

If, on the other hand, your children have been entitled, their chances of successfully leading your business in the future have been seriously compromised. You should carefully reorient them to the business facts of life described herein to achieve major reconstruction of their personal and professional values and/or move on to alternative sources of leadership (and ownership) successors.

Your children *must* earn their way into your business, and they can and should put their skin in the game. Do not keep thinking that they cannot purchase their ownership, because they can. Their paying forward is essential for the future health of the business and to their individual professional success.

If you are skeptical about the information in the above paragraphs and feel, for example, that your children cannot afford to purchase ownership, visit our website, www.spinnakerleadership.com, and tell us about your concern. We will be glad to help you.

2. **Misunderstood professional passions; forced career paths:**

Children of business founders often hear that they will someday replace the founder and own the business. This practice should be avoided. It fosters an entitlement mentality and an implicit or explicit directive that the children

will work for the business. What if your children do not want to work for your business but have not yet so informed you?

For example, as the founder of a successful restaurant, you may be happy to be identified and to find widespread respect as the best chef, with the best restaurant in town (that provides wealth for you and your family). Meanwhile, your children may be passionate about completely different professional areas—other than leading your business. Or they may see only that your long hours at the restaurant took you away from them and they do not want to do that to their children. Consequently, they will seek their identity and recognition in other business areas.

If, however, your children feel obligated to work in your business, they may comply, but they will lack the passion for and commitment to your business that are fundamental requirements for success. They will then most likely seek opportunities other than your business to achieve their professional goals for respect, reward, and self-esteem. Count on this and (discreetly) act accordingly.

Unfortunately, you may be (and probably will be) the last person to know how your children feel about running your business. They are reluctant to speak up. They probably believe that you do not want to hear that they are not interested in your business. They may be concerned that being candid and honest might hurt their parents' feelings and, maybe more importantly, could shut down an outstanding source of (unearned) respect and recognition, luxurious compensation, and lavish entitlements. Often, therefore, open communication on something so critical to the business and the family does not occur.

Consider these examples:

1. A management member of a family business told us that, in the same week that she had interviewed for and accepted a new job in a different company and city, her dad had begun telling customers of his business that she was his future successor. When she heard what he had done, she was unhappy but decided to withdraw from the new opportunity and stay in the family business ... for what now seems to her to be a lifelong solitary confinement. Even to the day of his death she did not tell her father of her career aspirations or the dream opportunity she rejected to comply with his wishes.

2. A first-generation leader of a large, successful, family business conglomerate asked us to assist his second-generation leaders. During an initial, one-on-one, confidential meeting, his son confided that he had saved $3 to $4 million and asked if that was enough to start an operation to successfully compete with his father's global business. The son added that he thought (incorrectly) that many of the current employees would go with him to his new business—thus he could start his business with identified target customers and experienced employees.

When asked where he managed to get $3 to $4 million at such a young age, he commented that the money came from his (excessive) compensation and trust fund distributions.

The son obviously did not fully appreciate who established his compensation level and who started and funded the trust fund. We suggested to him that with a global business and a substantial cash reserve, his father could probably crush *any* competitive startup business. We also reminded him that our company was hired by his father to teach him how to lead. We also asked him what of this conversation we should share with his father in a meeting scheduled for later the same day, and suggested that he should tell his father about what he really wanted to do.

3. An owner of a medium-size East Coast family business was absolutely certain that the youngest of his three sons would be his successor. However, in professionally facilitated, confidential leadership personality evaluation sessions and one-on-one interviews, the chosen son showed serious, irreparable leadership shortcomings and was not the best-qualified candidate.

    Equally important, the chosen son stated strongly during the evaluation sessions that he wanted nothing to do with the family business. Instead, he had his sights set on someday owning a distribution company in Colorado (where the snow skiing is fantastic). Significantly, he had never discussed his career aspirations with his father.

    How could Dad be so misinformed? Because dynamic, aggressive individuals who are busy creating and running their own businesses love their business creations and just cannot fathom that their children could see it any other way. They often make such statements as, "You will run this business, right?" or, "One day, this will all be yours." Such statements serve to bind the son or daughter to the business, no matter what may be their own professional passions.

The son did not have the gumption to be honest with his father about career aspirations, and, for reasons already discussed, he did not want to rock the "entitlement" boat.

4. During our first confidential meeting, a second-generation leader of his dad's global business requested a personal favor—would we ask for and orchestrate a salary increase for him from his father? He indicated that he was having great difficulty making ends meet. We responded that we understood that his annual compensation exceeded seven figures and that he also received substantial annual dividends from trust funds; therefore, we could not understand why it was difficult for him to make ends meet. We suggested that he address this need directly with his father.

Do these examples sound to you like leaders who are fully qualified and motivated to lead their parent's business to future success? Of course not. But you may be surprised to learn how often these and similar entitlement scenarios are present in family businesses. Is it any wonder that so many second-generation-led businesses fail?

Does your business harbor any of the pitfalls of these examples? If you answer no, how can you be so sure?

Almost everyone wants to create his or her own identity in life. Your business has given you personal satisfaction and an identity that makes you proud. Your business probably won't do that for your children as well as it has done it for you, *if at all*.

Wanting to follow their professional passions and create their own identity, members of the second generation would often rather do almost anything *except* run their parents' business.

Therefore, if your children feel a family obligation to work in your business, they will use all available resources to concurrently create their own business (even businesses competitive to yours) or attempt to diversify your business into what can provide them their own individual identity. Then, good luck to your business.

If a family member is not interested in potential leadership positions within the family business, that person should be able to discuss his or her ambitions openly and be graciously supported in the pursuit of his or her professional dreams. Give your children the opportunity and support to choose their own career path, as objectively you would do for them if you were employed somewhere and did not have your own business.

3. **Ineffective delegation:**

Many family business founders would "rather do it themselves"; delegation is not a practiced habit. Consequently, the second generation (children or other employees) is not as deeply involved in the key elements of the business as is desirable for enhancing their leadership impact and maximizing chances for future success.

In chapter 7 we discuss using your delegation capability as an effective leadership succession tool. Through expanded use of delegation you can also enhance your leadership impact and the impact of your team and provide maximum support for the leadership growth of your second generation.

4. Choosing the "most qualified" of your children:

Most founders seek to appoint one of their children as their successor (probably not the best idea), often for the wrong reasons. For example, the reasons often include first born or first-born son. Sometimes the chosen child is not the most qualified one but is the one that looks most like the founder. (We're not making this up.)

Also, unfortunately and foolishly, the future leadership selection is often made for the wrong reasons when the children are too young. For example:

> A large, world-class sports business owner once escorted his four-year-old great-grandson onto a major event stage and introduced the young boy as the fourth-generation leader of the national business. That's a small ego-trip for great-granddad, but it ignores the young boy's as yet unknown future aspirations, capabilities and special talents.

Sometimes, the founder of a family business goes to the trouble of determining (subjectively) which of his children is most qualified. Unfortunately, although this sounds good, this approach has fundamental flaws.

Choosing between siblings assumes that the chosen one actually has the skills and passion for the business, which, as we have discussed, is unlikely. Choosing between siblings also assumes that the most qualified offspring is the most qualified candidate available anywhere, which also is unlikely.

These assumptions automatically preclude searching for the most qualified candidate from a much-broader pool of candidates and often lead to selection of unqualified or mediocre successor candidates.

Focusing only on direct descendants also demotivates talented, committed, nonfamily member employees who perceive that birthright is *the* essential qualification for advancement.

As will be discussed in chapter 9, use a broad pool of candidates for identifying outstanding potential leadership successors for positions throughout your business. Develop and implement a practical leadership succession plan. Consider professional help in creating your plan and in selecting leadership successors that will propel your business forward through the current and future generations.

5. Use of trust structures for ownership succession:

Use of trust structures is one of many ownership succession options to protect assets and control estate taxes. However, trust structures are often

- conducive to a leadership-devastating entitlement culture within the next generation,
- focused almost solely on estate planning,
- not well understood by the business owner,
- implemented confidentially with legal and accounting advisors but with little or no communication with the next generation,
- a basic conflict of interest between the needs/welfare of the family and a trust fund advisor, who often becomes a trustee of the trust fund, and
- cumbersome and expensive to start and maintain.

Since trust funds engender an entitlement mind-set for the beneficiaries (usually the founders' children), trust funds can be toxic to effective leadership succession. For this reason alone, trust funds should not be implemented as a primary ownership succession tool.

Alternatives to trust funds can accomplish essentially the same asset and tax management objectives and provide other benefits without the negative consequences of trust funds. Alternatives to trust funds are discussed in our forthcoming book, **Family Business: Practical Ownership Succession Planning**. Meanwhile, should you have questions or want additional information, contact Spinnaker Leadership Associates, Inc., www.spinnakerleadership.com.

6. **The second-generation members are not capable, committed, or motivated to lead the business:**

See chapters 7, 8, 9, 10, 11, and 12 for corrective suggestions.

7. **Founders often use the business to provide a job and a lifestyle level for which the children are not qualified:**

Our experience is that the most common reasons for selecting one of the children to lead the business is to ensure that (1) he or she has a well-paying job and (2) control of the business stays in the family. These are good causes in and of themselves but poor reasons for this decision.

This parental caring for children who cannot hold the same pay scale job in another business or who are not able to sufficiently provide for themselves is understandable. But you should retain that challenge as a parental responsibility. Although you may wish it to be so, it is not a productive responsibility of your business or its employees to carry the lifestyle load of your children.

Maintaining control of the family business and employing children are separate objectives and should be addressed separately. Maintaining control can be accomplished without appointing children as future leaders.

8. **Owners want to make their children (and other employees) "happy":**

It is important to realize that happiness comes from within and is difficult or impossible to be created and provided by others. An attempt to create happiness (empowering others) often results in unnecessary entitlements (especially for family members) that damage commitment and motivation.

Create and nurture a performance-oriented, challenging environment (chapter 11), and your employees will be more inclined to respect—and want to work for—your business.

How your children have been treated (have they been entitled or not) as prospective employees or as actual employees will determine if they will be motivated by a performance-oriented, challenging environment.

9. **Job responsibilities and accountability are unclear or not articulated. The strategic business plan is inadequate, and priorities are not cascaded (delegated through each level) and communicated throughout the organization:**

    Job descriptions are discussed in chapter 8. If you need additional assistance with job descriptions or creating an effective business plan, contact Spinnaker Leadership Associates, Inc., www.spinnakerleadership.com.

10. **Ownership succession, rather than leadership succession planning, has been implemented and includes derailers for practical leadership succession:**

Our suggestions in chapters 1, 3, 4 and 5 will help remedy this issue.

11. **Family business owners have too little information or are confused about how to create and implement practical and effective leadership succession:**

Our suggestions in this book will help remedy this issue.

12. **Advice from trusted friends or advisors is misinformed or ineffective:**

Family business founders often hold onto relationships with their early advisors and, as the business grows, extend that relationship into areas for which the advisors have insufficient experience.

Consider this example:

> For a number of good reasons, we suggested to a new client that he consider the use of nonvoting stock in his Subchapter S family business corporate structure. His longtime family attorney responded to our client that it was not legal to structure nonvoting stock in a Subchapter S corporate structure. He may have been

confusing the use of two classes of stock (not allowed in Subchapter S corporate structures) with voting and nonvoting stock. Much time and money was wasted in educating this misinformed legal advisor, who may be a good attorney but apparently did not understand corporate structures.

Business founders may ask for opinions from a number of different advisors that are unskilled or semiskilled in the subject, causing continual confusion. Asking a general practitioner or a number of general practitioners may work for the advisors, but, like asking family doctors to do brain surgery, it may not provide the best service to the owner or the business.

Raise the bar and seek help from professional leadership and leadership succession specialists to ensure the highest level of effectiveness and efficiency.

13. The owner's exit strategy is undefined, confusing, or unspoken to others:

Read chapter 7 and define your exit strategy and timing and do it well, early. Confidentially communicate your exit strategy to those it will affect. Keeping it a secret from them is an idea that limits your options and resources for leadership succession.

14. **Business cash flow is already insufficient to carry the ever-increasing family overhead load:**

    If insufficient cash flow is a challenge for you, contact Spinnaker Leadership Associates, Inc., www.spinnakerleadership.com.

15. **Business and leadership training is inadequate:**

    If you have questions or need assistance, contact Spinnaker Leadership Associates, Inc., www.spinnakerleadership.com.

Consider the significance of the above list of leadership succession derailers and business destroyers on the future of your business.

Personalize and prioritize the list for your focused attention as you read on, and formulate corrective actions accordingly.

Chapter 7

Effective Delegation: An Exciting Leadership Succession Tool

"Leaders don't create followers, they create more leaders."

—Tom Peters

Leadership succession is stigmatized because it is frequently premised on the exit or demise of the current leader—and the leader wants no part of either premise. And, all too often, leadership succession is implemented as an event rather than an ongoing process.

Instead, leadership succession should be implemented as an ongoing process of ever-increasingly effective delegation—cascading responsibilities through each level.

Effective delegation is when the person to whom you delegate is fully vetted as capable for the responsibility, and you have communicated clearly and in advance what you specifically expect, when it is expected, what level of accomplishment is acceptable, and any related incentives or consequences.

Through effective delegation you can develop leaders throughout your organization—even if in their formal responsibility they only influence but do not supervise others. This creates a natural, seamless process that (1) leverages your talents, (2) magnifies your accomplishments, (3) enables you to be a more effective and more successful leader, and (4) will simplify and enhance leadership succession. Through continuous, effective delegation, top leadership succession can be achieved with relative ease. For example, if over time you could delegate all of your key leadership functions, then at some point leadership succession will be complete without much fuss. Yes?

In chapter 1 you read an example of the devastation that insufficient delegating can engender. On the flip side, those family business leaders who delegate effectively often enjoy a much higher level of professional leadership effectiveness as well as significantly more ease and progress with leadership succession And, should something unexpected happen, like incapacitation or death of the founder—or other family tragedy—a seamless, practical leadership succession can be implemented.

On the cusp of retirement or death, many of our clients have expressed that they wished they had spent more time with their family or on their exciting hobbies. But not many entering retirement or anticipating death have expressed a wish that they had spent more time on their business.

Does it really make sense to work so hard 24/7 to create, lead, and grow a business until time erases whatever else life could have offered you? No, it does not.

So why do so many family business founders do it? Are they just masochistic? Do they need the business more than it needs them? Are they unable to delegate? Is there no one to whom they can comfortably delegate? Or are all these causes working simultaneously?

Why not reverse the typical approach of working hard and planning for retirement at sixty-five or seventy and, instead, place high priority on effective delegation, to enhance your leadership impact and your business success early in life, while you can still enjoy other exciting activities along the way—and while you mentor future succession candidates to higher levels of success?

As you read in chapters 4, 5, and 6, the chances of your children successfully leading your business in the future are slim. Even if they have interest in leading your business someday, which statistically is unlikely, they probably won't wait until you are ready to delegate leadership authority to them. And if they do wait, they will probably want to change the business to apply their personal signature, which might seriously jeopardize your business.

If you start your enhanced delegating approach now, your children may not yet be ready to receive your delegated responsibilities. Don't worry about that. **Take care of your business and you.** Find the people to whom you can delegate effectively and get on with it. If in the future your children become qualified to accept leadership responsibilities, you can consider including them at that time and making changes accordingly.

You may be thinking, "But I can't do it; the business needs me 24/7." If you *really* believe that, please reread the example in chapter 1. Did you notice that part about the pandemonium caused by insufficient delegation or that the business is likely to fail due to the lack of a leadership succession plan and the presence of an ill-conceived ownership succession plan? The owner inadvertently abdicated a prime leadership responsibility—planning for the future prosperity and survival of the business (possibly while trying to pamper and protect his children)—by not delegating effectively while moving his priorities from the tactical to the strategic. One could also question if the strain of doing everything himself accelerated his death.

Abdication of leadership through ineffective or incomplete delegation occurs when you ambiguously tell someone to do something without fully vetting the qualifications of the delegate or without providing clarity of expectations, directions, metric parameters, and timing. This abdication is a serious, negative leadership characteristic. It facilitates poor performance. It also enables the abdicator to subsequently criticize (and demotivate) the delegate for lack of acceptable performance, even though the absence of clear communication at the onset may have caused the unacceptable outcome. Consider this example:

A new client had worked 24/7 (note: *no* time off) for five years to turn around his struggling California electronics company. One Friday he decided to take a few hours off with his family in wine country and asked his production manager to take charge in his absence. He reasonably assumed that she knew about and would make the overdue shipments important to cash flow before the end of the day. However, when he called the business number at about 4:00 p.m. there was no answer. When he reached a design engineer on a direct line, he was told that everyone had been dismissed for the day, and the factory was closed at 1:30 p.m.—half an hour after the owner had left the building. His production manager later told him that, since it was a sunny California Friday afternoon and since he had taken off early, she gave everyone else the afternoon off even though none of the shipments had been made.

He fired her. But he could not make the late shipments arrive on time. This experience was an expensive lesson about leadership succession and the role of effective delegation.

Delegating effectively may save your business, your life, or both. And if you delegate effectively, reprioritizing your time for the most important things while leading your business successfully will become straightforward.

Effective delegation will magnify your leadership impact and can become the lifeblood of your leadership succession planning.

Just as you would seek professional help to learn to play the violin, consider professional help to fully develop and implement your delegating skills—they are the most important part of your leadership skills.

Meanwhile, the following steps should help you delegate more effectively:

1. Prepare a detailed description for your job (See chapter 8). Clearly delineate the key areas of your responsibilities and functions; for example, rainmaker (getting new orders), new business development, maintenance sales, operations leadership, financial planning, cost control, human resource management, marketing planning, community relationships, supplier leadership, etc. Give priority to quality over brevity in the content of the document.

2. Following the suggestions outlined in chapter 8, cascade part or all of your job's responsibilities and functions to the appropriate subordinate job descriptions. Much of your

rainmaking responsibility, for example, may fit best in the sales manager job description.

3. Cascade each responsibility and function to lower-level positions without being influenced by the capabilities of the person in the job. *It's about getting the responsibility into the logically right job, not about the person in the job.*

4. Recruit, train or replace as needed so that those in jobs with delegated responsibilities become fully qualified "stand-ins," to take individual responsibility for specific elements cascaded from your job description.

5. Seek a replacement immediately if you have the wrong person in the job. For example, if you cannot cascade your rainmaking function into your sales manager job description because your sales manager will not or cannot carry out the function acceptably, you need a new sales manager.

6. Assign (it's called delegating) more and more of your key job elements to your "stand-in" subordinates for increasingly longer and more frequent periods (for example, short offsite business meetings graduating to monthlong business or personal trips).

7. Provide specific instructions about how and for what you want to be interrupted while you are focused on other activities. Then check in on a predetermined schedule for brief updates. For example, if you want your e-mail and snail mail managed while you are gone for a week, you must describe what you want done with the issues in your mail, by whom and by when, and the follow-up you expect to hear about or do not want to be involved in, and ensure that each individual is prepared to meet your expectations.

   If you want phone calls and all matters resolved before you return, communicate this expectation early and clearly. Ensure that those to whom you are delegating can actually carry out (are fully equipped to do it, have proper level of authority, etc.) your direction.

8. Observe how well your job functions are carried out while you are gone, and provide continual feedback to enhance future results to the point where you can be gone for long periods of time without frequent, unnecessary interruptions of your schedule or jeopardizing the health of your business.

9. As this process starts to work well, continue the cascading process of each level to the next lower job level.

Some caveats:

- Using this delegation approach does not mean (nor should they be told it means) that the temporary "stand-ins" will be your future leadership successor candidates. It means that you are enhancing your leadership impact and the effectiveness of your professional and personal lives while (discreetly) learning how to identify **potential** leadership candidates at all levels in your business.
- Allow your children to participate in this program only if they are sincerely interested and fully qualified to act as a "stand-in". Do not use this approach as learn-on-the-job training for them. Doing so demeans other employees' jobs and, once again, communicates that your children are "special" employees.
- Your children may be qualified candidates for jobs that receive these added responsibilities. However, if they are not willing, qualified, and ready, don't wait— place others in these jobs and proceed accordingly. This approach enables you to see how others perform and reinforces to your children that only if and when they become interested and fully qualified as the best candidate for the job may they become successor

candidates. Meanwhile, if they are employed in the family business, they should be compensated and treated according to policies that are suggested in chapters 11 and 12.

- Find and recruit the most qualified and capable individuals for your business and for candidates to potentially succeed you. Prepare yourself (and act accordingly) for the reality that the most qualified, interested, and motivated candidates for this program will probably not be your children. Use your business head, not your parental conscience, for this critical element of your leadership responsibility. This is how you would do it if you had purchased a business that already employed the previous owner's children, yes?

When you have successfully accomplished an effective delegation capability and process and have identified competent "stand-ins," you will have (1) enhanced your leadership skills, (2) freed up valuable time for more strategic or other activities versus tactical functions, (3) created a bench of potential successors for middle-management or top leadership positions, and (4) better prepared yourself and others for a future, effective, practical leadership succession.

Chapter 8

Job Descriptions: A Key Step to Leadership Success and Practical Leadership Succession

The employment needs of the business, not the number or needs of employees, nor the number or needs of one's family members, determine the number, types, and contents of leadership and other positions required by the business.

Please read that again if you have difficulty becoming a believer.

To clearly articulate the employment needs of the business, job descriptions should be created for **every** job, starting with the top position. Each job description must be comprehensive in its depiction of key job responsibilities and duties and inclusive of all applicable required qualifications. Quality of the content of the job description is important, brevity is not.

Use a zero-based approach to quantify and confirm each of the employment needs of the company and the number, types, and contents of required jobs. Don't accept input of "that's how it's always been done here" or "Harry has been in that job for fifteen years; he knows what to do."

The job description is not just a piece of bureaucratic paperwork. It is the orator of what is required from each job to help the business and the qualified individual in the job to be successful.

The job description is also the standard against which the qualifications and capabilities of each job candidate and employee can be measured for employment decisions, performance appraisals, and compensation levels.

The content of the job description should *not* be influenced by the capabilities, qualifications, performance, or needs of the individual in the job or a candidate for the job. Each job description must stand alone, unrelated to the person who is or may be placed in the job.

A sample job description for the position of chief executive officer of Company X is provided in exhibit 3 and can be used as a starting job description template for your position.

You should expand or modify this sample job description template to include content specific to each job in your business, to add your personal business touch, and to include required legal stipulations from federal, state, and local governments.

When the description for the top-level job is complete, repeat the process for each successive lower-level position. Start by appropriately cascading each of the duties and responsibilities of the top-level job description into each respective next lower-level job, and then add the more specific duties and responsibilities of the lower-level job. For example, the top leadership job description might say, "Leads competitive strategies ..." The job description for the top sales manager job then might say, "Assists the chief executive officer to lead, develop, and implement competitive strategies within the sales department ..."

Continue the cascading process to create current, comprehensive job descriptions for every job in your business.

Communicate the duties, responsibilities, and qualification requirements of each position to all employees as appropriate. This is a key step in ensuring that family members and other key employees understand what is expected for each position, especially positions that they aspire to someday hold for the business.

Exhibit 3

Job Description Template: Chief Executive Officer Company X Inc.

Job Description: Chief Executive Officer

Reports to: The owners (or board of directors) of Company X Inc.

Summary:

The chief executive officer of the company has leadership authority for all aspects of general management and affairs of the corporation and shall perform all duties and have all powers that are commonly incident to the position of chief executive officer or which are delegated to the position by the owners of the company, the board of directors, or the corporate articles and bylaws.

The chief executive officer is responsible for

- developing, implementing, and communicating the corporate vision, mission statement, and values;
- strategic plans;

- all aspects of company operations;
- budgets;
- financial performance results;
- near- and long-term corporate health;
- internal and external relationships;
- employee recruitment, hiring, firing, and motivation;
- compensation policies, plans, and procedures;
- corporate image;
- risk management;
- investment goals and management;
- working capital; and
- shareholder investment return.

The chief executive officer has general supervisory authority to lead all other officers, employees, and agents of the corporation, to delegate as and when appropriate, and to accomplish company objectives with effectiveness, efficiency, and professionalism.

The chief executive officer has authority to sign all stock certificates, contracts, investment and banking documents, financial asset and liability instruments, and other documents that are authorized by the owners or the company, the board of directors or the corporate articles and bylaws.

The chief executive officer is a member of the board of directors of Company X Inc. (if there is a board of directors and if this position is a part of the board of directors).

Job Responsibilities and Duties:

Leads the corporate culture, strategic direction, and foundation of all company activities, including but not limited to, customer relationships and commitments; employee hiring and firing; training, productivity, appraisal plans, promotional policies, and succession programs; the management of compensation and incentive plans; pricing plans and practices; purchasing; vendor relationships; asset purchases and liability management; site engagement and management; community relationships and interactions; company policies, practices and procedures, and philanthropy

Leads the development, implementation, commitment to, and communication of our values, vision, mission, priorities, policies, practices, principles, and procedures

Leads the representation of Company X Inc. to our customers, employees, vendors, neighbors, and community, with the highest level of integrity and professionalism

Supervises all employees directly or through permanent or temporary management teams

Generates and leads a culture in which employees are motivated to commit to, work for and otherwise assist Company X Inc. to have ever-increasing stability, growth, and financial success

Leads creation and development, and ensures the implementation of

- business and competitive strategies and tactics to meet corporate growth and financial objectives;
- annual and long-term planning, forecasting, budgeting, resourcing, and monitoring functions;
- revenue-generating strategies and tactics, pricing plans, customer services, and sales functions; and
- strategies and programs for cash flow optimization, investment, and financial security.

Develops, implements, and administers strategies and programs to optimize the lease, sale or acquisition, and use of corporate physical facilities and equipment

Leads creation, development, implementation, and monitoring of employee compensation and incentive compensation programs, benefit plans, and personnel policies and procedures

Is a visionary who leads by setting examples of excellence, commitment, urgency, effectiveness, efficiency, professionalism, attentiveness, accountability, and safety

Develops, proposes, implements, and administers strategies and programs for mergers, acquisitions, and divestitures

Authority:

As described herein, has responsibility and commensurate authority defined by the owners or board of directors, corporate articles and bylaws, vision, mission, values, and policies to lead all aspects of company functions

Directly and indirectly leads approximately (X to Y) permanent and temporary employees plus outside contractors in the various functions of Company X Inc.

Financial authority level is representative of that of a medium-size, privately held corporation, including an annual budget of approximately ($X to $Y)

Job Qualifications:

- High integrity
- Enthusiasm for and commitment to the corporation and its vision, mission, and values
- Visionary, effective leader with strong people skills
- Innovative thinker and self-starter with perseverance to lead teams to success
- Ability to weather adversity with graciousness while attending to the longer-term goals and priorities
- Effective communication skills
- Advanced skills and experience with all operations and management tools appropriate for the level of chief executive of a medium-size, privately held company
- Strong people skills
- Focus on and commitment to customer satisfaction and service

- Ability to develop and leverage effective relationships with user, community, industry, supplier, and media representatives
- Ability to delegate effectively and efficiently
- Capability for sincere interest in listening
- An objective and positive motivational leader
- Patience and graciousness
- Persistent follow-up
- Superior organizational skills
- Self-discipline, actualization, and achievement
- Sense of urgency; deadline consciousness and follow-up
- Strategic and tactical competitor
- College degree or high school diploma and applicable financial experience and leadership training

Work Environment and Physical Demands:

The work environment and physical demands of this position are representative of those in an office, residential, commercial, or industrial environment and local or long-distance driving by automobile and travel by bus, train, plane, or ship.

Reasonable accommodations may be made to enable individuals with disabilities to perform the essential functions of the job.

Date: _____

Authorized by: _____

Chapter 9

Selecting Leadership Successors; Practical Steps

"Bad people do not destroy an organization—we get rid of them.

But, mediocre people can destroy an organization."

—Bill Gates

Family business founders often choose one of their children to succeed them since (1) as parents, they want their offspring to have good lifestyles and (2) as business owners, they want control of the business to stay in the direct family. Often, this approach compromises leadership succession plans because the successor candidates are not the most qualified individuals and in many cases are only mediocre candidates.

Would the countries that compete for the America's Cup trophy choose only the most talented and qualified skippers and sailors for their specially designed yachts, or would they choose the children of previous competitors for their crew, even though they might be only mediocre sailors?

If family business founders considered all possible options and were unfettered and totally objective in searching for a successor, would the most qualified of their children be the most qualified available candidate for leading their businesses?

Hypothetically speaking, if you had sold your business, would the new owner choose any of your children as the most qualified candidate for your position ... from all of the available sources?

Accepting mediocre candidates for any job is unwise. Accepting mediocre, "birthright" candidates in leadership positions can quickly diminish the net value of the family enterprise and accelerate business failure. Selecting less than the most qualified successor for your replacement could even be catastrophic, depriving you and your family of the continuing rewards of a successful business. In that case, would you really have made the right decisions for the financial welfare of your children?

For any job in your business, the preferred candidate must be the most qualified individual for the job. What is best for the business will be best for the family, including members of future generations. A family member who is not the most qualified person for the job should not be put in the job unless and until he or she becomes the most qualified person for the job. **No exceptions.**

If you have constructed your job description as we discussed in chapter 8, congratulations. You have defined and articulated the responsibilities, duties, and qualifications of your job.

Now, take the next step. **Objectively** identify and quantify your personal leadership characteristics and qualifications—those strengths and special talents that enabled you to lead your business to success. Do this, also, for the weaknesses that have been barriers to success that you would like to avoid in a successor candidate. Then use this information along with your job description as your specification for considering and evaluating candidates to replace you.

Why? How? Consider the following example:

> In a recent client project, the strengths, special talents, and weaknesses of the business founder, an impressive leader, were identified and quantified. Most crucial to growing his

business from scratch to a global enterprise were his visionary talent, his market acumen, his conservative financial savvy, his commitment and stamina to business success, and his superior ability to network and to secure and retain business despite fierce competition and adversarial market conditions.

The project analyses showed also that the strengths and special talents of those adult children whom the founder considered to be the most likely leadership successor candidates were impressive. However, none of them appeared to have his visionary talent, his conservative financial savvy or his ability to network and to secure and retain business despite fierce competition and adversarial market conditions. And, in fact, the key successor candidates had innate weaknesses that could seriously impede effective, long-lasting customer relationships.

So critical elements of the success of the business would be missing if and when the founder appointed one of his children to succeed him. Therefore, (1) his children should *not* be candidates to succeed him (preferred choice), or (2) candidates with the critical elements of success must be found and added to the top-level team before a leadership succession plan is implemented.

How do you objectively identify and quantify your strengths, special talents, and weaknesses? Take the time to stand back and objectively evaluate yourself—confirm and document your strengths, special talents and weaknesses. You might ask for help from those who know you well and have the courage to be open, objective, and critical.

Better yet, seek help from proven professionals. This choice is usually the most efficient and effective approach.

When looking for your successor, consider at least the following possible sources and be objective, thorough and consistent in your evaluations before you select your preferred options:

1. Direct descendants
2. Extended family members
3. Experienced leadership professionals from within and outside your business
4. Acquisition of or merger with a compatible business that has fully qualified leadership in place to take the combined business forward expeditiously and successfully to a higher level

5. Sale of your business while it is at its peak value, to employees or others, and using the proceeds to fund your and your family's future professional adventures

Naturally, you may be reluctant to consider candidates other than your children for your replacement. But remember that:

1. The business is yours—it is not your children's business.
2. Their professional passions might not (likely will not) be aligned with your professional passion.
3. Your children may not, in fact, have the capabilities and talents needed to carry out your leadership functions as well as you do.
4. By considering other qualified candidates, you can measure the pros and cons of the qualifications of your children with more objectivity.
5. Your children's welfare may be better served if they are employees and/or shareholders rather than leaders of your business.

Communicate with your children well in advance about your intention to consider *all* logical sources of leadership candidates to identify your successor. Make it clear that, for the best care of the business and, therefore, the best care of the family, only the most qualified person will get the job. Make it clear, also, that birthright may influence but will not drive the decision, and, if they are interested in the job, they need to be or become the most qualified candidate for the opening and demonstrate their interest and commitment. Make it clear also that, should they want to become shareholders, financial commitment will be necessary.

This approach encourages frank communication about your children's professional qualifications, aspirations, and passions so you can better understand and support them. And, when they feel that you actually welcome their unencumbered input, they will be more candid about their professional aspirations.

If your children are not very interested, not qualified, or are still too young to be considered as leadership candidates, find leadership candidates elsewhere and place them as needed to create a leadership bench. And, as we discussed in chapters 7 and 8, cascade (delegate) your responsibilities, so you can leverage your talents, enhance your leadership impact, and enjoy a more effective life while your practical leadership plan is being developed and implemented. Continue this process until your leadership succession has been accomplished.

While following the above advice, address and solve any familial challenges that may occur. For example, suppose you are considering hiring an outside, experienced leadership professional as your successor, and you are concerned about how your children may react. Start early with them to help them develop their best career path, within or outside (preferably outside) of your business.

Some advisors encourage the use of a board of directors to develop a leadership succession plan and to identify successors. This approach may appear attractive in that it might "lighten your load" of choosing between siblings. But there are significant downside risks. For example, the use of a board of directors may impede open communication between you and your children about future leadership decisions. Also, it could show your cowardice (the second generation is smart, right?) in abdicating your responsibility of choosing a successor.

Incidentally, when someone suggests an outside board of directors for any reason, be sure to re-review the articles of incorporation and bylaws of your business structure to fully understand the pros and cons of an outside board of directors.

And, until you are better informed, disregard this suggestion and run like a scalded dog. You built and you own your family business. You do not need a fixed set of outside bosses to manage you, to separate you from your responsibilities and the freedoms of running your business, or to get between you and your children on any matters related to your business.

There are professional advisors who specialize in identifying the strengths, special talents, and weaknesses of leadership successor candidates and who can assist you to hire the most qualified candidate. Use of such professional advisors makes sense in that it facilitates the leadership succession process while optimizing the use of your time. But this works well only if (1) the advisors are proven experts in leadership succession, (2) they bring important and practical information that you need, (3) their arrangement is focused and temporary, and (4) **you personally lead the effort**.

When evaluating candidates to replace you, answer at least the following questions:

1. Do the potential successor candidates have the best combination of qualifications, strengths, and special talents to replace you?

Which of your strengths are critical to the success of your business? An example is rainmaking—creating the revenues. Most founders are good at rainmaking. They had to be to get the business to success. Unfortunately, this strength is often missing in the second generation and, therefore, not available when the founder leaves the business. If creating revenues is one of your talents, your replacement must be similarly talented or someone else must pick up this slack ... or your business will suffer.

2. Are the potential successor candidates fully qualified for the top job?

Qualifying for your job requires having the maturity and experiences to lead, the capabilities to meet all other requirements depicted in the top leader's job description, and the commitment and stamina needed to meet the challenges of the position. These characteristics and capabilities can be observed in how an individual performs in lower-level jobs and in personal life activities. Even better, These characteristics can be quantified through the use of professional counsel using professionally structured evaluations, interviews, resumes, and reference checks.

3. Are the potential successor candidates committed and motivated to make your business as successful as possible?

Commitment and motivation are based on personal values, professional passions, qualifications, fortitude, and expectations. For example, you find satisfaction and excitement in what you do. You are passionate about and committed to your family business. When you started your business, you perceived that you could lead it to success. Your expectations included, among other things, (1) gaining respect for your persistence and accomplishment of creating a successful business and (2) establishing a comfortable lifestyle for you and your family. How will potential leadership successor candidates view the opportunity to lead your business? Are their values and professional passions aligned with yours?

Summary:

To evaluate appropriate finalist candidates for leadership positions, it is important to have a clear, unbiased understanding of each candidate's strengths, weaknesses, special talents, demonstrated performance levels, qualifications, and, equally important, professional passions and career aspirations.

This information, plus how well a candidate's strengths and special talents match yours, and how many of your pertinent weaknesses the candidate can overcome, can determine the future success of your business.

The following steps can assist you in identifying, evaluating, and selecting your successor:

1. Seek help as needed from qualified professionals.
2. Confirm and document your values, strengths, special talents, weaknesses, professional passions, and key functional responsibilities. Use this information and the job description for your position as a template for successor evaluations.
3. Define and document the values, strengths, weaknesses, special talents, professional passions and experiences (positive and negative experiences) of each leadership candidate.
4. Thoroughly vet each candidate's capabilities, experiences, and readiness against the written leadership job description and industry standards. Be sure not to compromise the requirements of the position description as you evaluate each candidate.

5. Confirm that each leadership candidate's values, professional passions, and actual (versus theoretical) level of interest in, commitment to, and experiences for the job align with your expectations for someone who will be the top leader of your business.
6. Involve members of the second-generation family and selected employees in the candidate evaluation process to get their feedback and to expose them to the quality of the talent you are considering.
7. Use the information from Nos. 1 through 6 to facilitate the qualification and selection process.
8. Personally check references (in face-to-face meetings, if at all possible) thoroughly before making any leadership or other key appointments.

Chapter 10

Helping Your Children Find Their Professional Passions

"Example is not the main thing in influencing others, it is the only thing."

—Albert Schweitzer

To enhance your children's chances of being successful in life, consider the following:

1. Give your children priority over the business. Business opportunities have many lives, but you only get to spend a short amount of your children's lives with them. Be there for them even when you think your business needs you more. If your business keeps getting in the way, you may need professional guidance to increase your leadership impact and capabilities and to realign your priorities.

2. If, even with professional help, you cannot spend quality time with your children and concurrently run your business successfully, you have the wrong professional help. Or, apparently, you are not up to your leadership challenges. If you continue on this path, it is likely you will someday lose the business or the children or both.

3. Take sincere interest in your children and spend quality time with them. The quality time you spend with them helps to develop who they will be and their strengths and special talents. Spending quality time with them also helps you to better understand the values, capabilities, and individual passions and aspirations of each child.

4. Make it a priority to learn what your children's interests are—even their fashionable interests of the moment—and support their passion explorations at every opportunity. If your daughter wants you to take her fishing, even if fishing is "not your thing," what are you waiting for? This helps you to nurture her and her interests and to learn more about her aspirations, passions, strengths, and special talents.

5. Turn off your cell phone and do not be distracted by your business (cell phone, e-mail, conversations, etc.) when

you are with your children. That's not quality time; it's demonstrating to them that they are secondary to your business. It also demonstrates your leadership weaknesses and negatively affects their opinion of your business.

6. Resist the temptation to tell your children or anyone else that your Mary or John will someday own your business or will someday replace you.

7. Do not complain about any aspect of your business to or in front of your children, for any reason.

8. If and when your children show genuine interest, tell them about what you do and what your business does. Tell them why what you do is exciting to you. If appropriate, take opportunities to visit their schools and talk about, for example, the "good parts" of leading a business.

9. When they are interested, tell your children more about the business and what it does for you, your family, and your community.

10. Do not drive your children toward a certain professional passion, particularly if you think that it will help them to one day lead the family business. What professional area they

become seriously passionate about, not what you think they should be passionate about, is what will ultimately drive them. Their professional decision-making processes should be supported, and their decisions should be respected.

11. Suggest employment in other businesses aligned with opportunities to explore and grow your children's professional interests. This enables them to explore their interests and get a perspective of how other businesses operate while they continue to grow.

12. If your children have interest in working for your business, **hire them only into jobs for which they are fully (and the most) qualified**.

13. If and while employed by your business, your children should be treated as you treat other employees, except that you should raise their performance bar higher than that for other employees and pay them less (chapters 11 and 12).

Chapter 11

Creating Commitment and Motivation in a Performance-Oriented Culture

> "Empowerment comes from within, it is an individual accomplishment. Leaders cannot empower, they can only provide the environment for others to empower themselves."
>
> —James F. Bracher

As discussed in chapter 5, commitment and motivation are essentially automatic during the first generation of a family business. The founders are committed to a vision and motivated by passion, pride, survival instincts, and the entrepreneurial drive to have their dream succeed.

As the number of employees increases and as family members are employed, commitment and motivation are not automatic and must be created and continually nurtured. Most employees want to be successful, but they do not naturally have the same passion, pride, or drive as you do to make your business succeed. This is especially true for second-generation family employees, who often have their own professional passions and may even dislike your business. They may perceive that the business distracted their parents from paying attention to the family.

An employee's motivation to succeed can be stymied by ineffective leadership that encourages or creates an entitlement mentality, mismatches job assignments to personal capabilities, offers unclear business priorities, or focuses on happiness instead of challenge, commitment, and motivation. Effective leadership can remedy these issues and, when coupled with the employee's initiative, can produce impressive results.

Eleven Key Steps to Successful Employee Commitment and Motivation:

Give serious consideration to the following key steps to successful employee commitment and motivation.

Step No.11, "Incentives for Employees—Partners in Success," is particularly important. It discusses effective and efficient incentives versus more "fashionable" but less effective/more costly options that are often used.

1. Vision

The Vision statement is the cornerstone of the business plan, the origin of all priorities, and helps ensure that the work of each employee is meaningful and personally rewarding. Create and communicate a clear, concise statement of your *vision*—where you want the company to be going. Keep it simple—as few words as possible—so that each employee can easily repeat the *vision*. Ensure that each employee has a complete understanding of and makes a commitment to the *vision*.

Spinnaker Leadership's vision statement is "Preeminent Leadership," and we continuously strive to accomplish that for ourselves and for our clients.

2. Values

Define, communicate, and live your *Values*—what you stand for and how employees should treat each other, customers, vendors, and the community.

Spinnaker Leadership's Values include, for example, ***Integrity, Client Priority, Visionary anticipation, Leadership, Commitment, Excellence, Precision, Common Sense and Accountability.***

3. **Business Plan**

   Create a written business plan that details at least the key strategies, priorities, financing steps, industry and customer targets, competitive analyses, marketing strategies, sales forecasts, employment plans, and financial and cash flow projections.

4. **Priorities**

   Ensure that the business priorities, which derive from the ***Vision*** through the business plan, are well communicated to and understood by each employee. Cascade each of the key business priorities into the specific priorities of each job. This alignment helps ensure that the work of each employee is meaningful, thus engendering commitment and motivation.

5. Lead by Example

Leaders and family members must continually lead by example—demonstrating unwavering commitment to the **Vision**, **Values**, and **Priorities**. Treat all employees with respect and fairness, as you would want to be treated. Seek out and eradicate all inconsistencies that indicate one thing by word and another thing by action. No exceptions!

6. Frequent, Open Communication

Promote frequent, open communication. Employees want and deserve to know essential information, whether the news is good or bad. Essential information includes, for example, the **Vision**, **Values**, **Priorities**, and **Strategies**, as well as status of the business, key events, and accomplishments of individuals, teams, and the business.

Put yourself in your employee's shoes. Essential information includes anything that you, as an employee, would like to know to enhance your confidence in the business and its leader and to do your job more effectively.

7. Match Individual Capabilities to Job Requirements

Employees working to their full potential are usually well motivated. Quantitatively evaluate each employee's capabilities and match the employee's strengths to the job assignments. Provide training and development assistance to ensure that employees can be competent in their jobs and become qualified for new challenges.

8. Teamwork, Not Internal Competition

Internal competitive activity wastes resources, clouds priorities, dilutes focus, and negatively affects morale. Teamwork magnifies the effectiveness of employees and benefits productivity and performance, while increasing employee motivation and morale.

Foster teamwork through positive assignments, structures, and incentives. Reserve competitive energies for overcoming external threats to your business.

9. Career Development and Advancement

Understand the development and advancement desires of each employee. Provide and communicate clear paths and requirements to meet these needs. Where advancement is crucial but openings are unavailable, seek and implement creative and challenging opportunities for committed and motivated employees.

10. Accountability

Treat all employees with the same high standards of respect, commitment, motivation, responsibility, and accountability that you expect for yourself. Provide job descriptions and communicate priorities. Measure progress frequently, with immediate, informal feedback, and through formal, periodic appraisals designed to foster a sense of urgency, growth, productivity, results, and accountability.

11. Incentives for Employees—Partners in Success

In approximate order of importance to employees, our studies indicate that effective incentives include the following:

- "Thank you"—sincere, respectful recognition for a job well done
- Feedback—praise in public, chastise in private

- Money—a share of the value of accomplishments through incentives paid out frequently and as soon as possible after the accomplishment milestone
- Opportunities to demonstrate and be respected for special talents
- Opportunities for growth
- Development and training for existing or new project assignments, expanded responsibilities, and advancement
- Paid personal time off

Note that annual bonuses and share of equity are absent from our recommended list of incentives.

Annual bonuses, for example, in cash, perks, or 401(k) awards, can be an ego trip for the business leader but normally have a short impact life—from weeks prior to weeks after the award date. In addition, annual bonuses become expensive entitlements for which the impact diminishes without continuous increases in the size of the award. Our recommended incentive actions are significantly more effective and efficient than annual bonuses of any kind and have an ongoing self-enforcing lifetime.

Share of equity has some motivational value but is relatively inefficient and ineffective compared with our recommended incentive options. And share of equity has serious downside risks. Use our recommended incentive options to their fullest extent before you consider equity participation by employees.

If you are skeptical about the higher value of well planned, communicated and implemented, timely incentives versus the value of annual bonuses or equity, consider the job of restaurant server.

It's a tough, demanding job that pays at minimum wage level or less. Restaurant servers are on their feet for long periods and often meet hungry, grumpy, demanding, and rude customers. So why do servers smile, appear eager to serve and hurry from table to table, accomplishing a critical business priority? Why are they committed to the job and motivated to do it well?

They are motivated because they are incentivized by an immediate payment for a job done well. That's right, *tips*! Servers know in advance what is expected from them and what they can generally expect, consistent with how well the job is done. Their incentive is the amount of the tip paid at the time the service is provided.

Suppose that all of the daily tips in a restaurant were collected and pooled into a total annual amount distributed at year-end as an amount averaged over all servers, like a 401(k) or an annual bonus. Each such annual tip amount could be very large. But how strong might individual server commitment and motivation be, particularly in the middle of the year?

As a customer, would you rather provide a tip to a server or have the owner save it up for a year-end bonus award? Other than for temporarily enhancing his or her personal cash flow, what restaurant owner would say that distributing tips in equal portions as a year-end bonus to all servers is a great idea?

Summary:

1. Nurture a performance-oriented culture centered on your **Vision**, **Values**, and **Priorities**.
2. Communicate the business **Vision**, **Values**, **Priorities**, Strategies, Compensation plans, and Incentive programs well in advance and often, to ensure that employees know clearly and specifically what is expected from them, what they can expect, and when they can expect it.

3. Practice the recommended eleven key steps to successful employee commitment and motivation and, as appropriate, tie them directly to individual and team accomplishments aligned with priorities.

4. Focus on creating a positive, challenging environment wherein compensation structure and incentives encourage performance and results consistent with the business priorities. Avoid rewards, which quickly become entitlements, in favor of performance incentives that stimulate commitment and motivation.

Creating employee commitment and motivation in a performance-oriented culture is up to you. **Do it now** and experience how creative, effective, and productive motivated employees can be!

Chapter 12
Compensation and Incentives for Success

Compensation programs should be structured to encourage strong performance while minimizing unnecessary costs of time and money. Compensation programs should be communicated in advance—in honest, straightforward, easy-to-understand, clear statements of structure, expectations, timing, and results.

Effective compensation programs include well-founded wage or salary structures and timely incentive elements that encourage strong performance in each job.

Well-planned and implemented job descriptions (chapter 8) can provide a foundation for the wage or salary *compensation range* for each job. The responsibilities, performance requirements and qualifications depicted in the job descriptions can be compared with those for similar jobs in other businesses to determine competitive compensation ranges.

Paying more than is needed for a job—a common tendency of family businesses—wastes money and reduces operational competitiveness. Paying less than what is paid by other businesses for similar jobs demotivates productive employees and encourages them to seek employment elsewhere.

Comparisons of compensation ranges for each job should be done frequently enough to keep the information current. Such comparisons can be a DIY project by learning how and what other businesses pay for similar jobs. Industry associations and chambers of commerce can be helpful in getting this information. Professionally prepared, publicly available compensation surveys can also be informative.

Once the compensation range for each job has been determined, an individual's **specific wage or salary** within the compensation range—modified appropriately by the frequency and impact of any incentives being used—should be directly related to how well the employee performs against the requirements of the job.

Performance incentives (as discussed in chapter 11) should be included in your compensation plan to encourage each employee to exceed job expectations. Incentives should foster excellent performance. Under no circumstances should salary, wages or incentives support or reward undesired performance or incomplete or less-than-expected (expectations communicated in advance) results.

Family employees who have different job levels or responsibilities should be paid according to what their job pays, modified by their level of performance. Family employees should not be paid a certain wage or salary because they have certain birthrights or needs. To pay according to birthright privileges or needs is inconsistent with a performance-based culture, provides entitlements that derail leadership commitment and motivation, and, once known (count on it becoming known) by other employees, damages leadership credibility and employee morale.

For those family employees with future leadership potential, give serious consideration to expecting them to show leadership commitment early. For example, they should lead by example and demonstrate more quality and quantity than their job description may indicate while being paid less salary or wage than what their job level pays, augmented by appropriate milestone performance incentives. This helps to confirm their interest in and commitment to the business, and minimizes trends toward entitlement mentalities. If you include incentive compensation in their total compensation, your children can earn more than others do—if they are the top performers. In that case, since they are paid less salary or wage than their job level may warrant, they have clearly earned their lifestyle; it is not an entitlement.

For example, consider a three-part family employee compensation package for next generation future leadership candidates that consists of (1) the wage or salary range of their position, discounted by 10 to 20 percent, plus (2) incentive compensation based on personal accomplishments that could equal or exceed 10 to 20 percent of base compensation, plus (3) a timely share of the success (cash flow) of the family business. This is a much better approach than paying according to last name or lifestyle needs and has intrinsic values in fostering commitment and motivation, eradicating entitlements, and confirming which family member is sincerely interested in being a leader of a successful family business.

With the above structure in place, nonfamily employees will eventually understand that family members work harder than nonfamily employees do but are paid less than nonfamily employees in similar positions. Everyone can then better understand that birthright may have some privileges but being overpaid, being promoted, or being lazy are not three of them. As a result, employees will tend to have more respect for you and your children, and will be more motivated to help make your business and your family-member employees successful.

Consider this example:

> Employees of a small family business were asked recently about their reaction to the owner's daughter being promoted to a middle management job en route to someday succeed the founder. Each employee responded that she was already fully qualified, with the possible exception of her knowledge of the financial aspects of the business. They also volunteered a high regard for her, citing that she worked hard even though she was paid less than that for other middle managers. They said that her commitment and compensation reflected the *values* and conservative nature of the family leadership and that birthright did not outweigh

common sense. They expressed looking forward to her moving into higher levels of leadership once she became more astute with financial matters.

Summary:

Ensure that all employee communications about compensation and incentives are open, honest, straightforward, easy-to-understand, clear statements of structure, expectations, timing, and results.

Base your compensation program on job descriptions and comparisons with similar jobs in other businesses that compete for your employees.

Base individual compensation levels on individual performance versus job requirements.

Update your compensation program frequently to ensure that your compensation at each job level is competitive but not excessive.

Incentivize excellent performance and desired and expected results. Never support undesired performance or reward incomplete or unsatisfactory results.

Pay family member employees in accordance with the stipulations of your compensation program.

Encourage family member employees, especially future leadership candidates, to earn their way to success.

Chapter 13

Practical Leadership Succession Planning: Takeaways

Practical, effective leadership succession planning can be straightforward. It just requires objectivity, commitment, mental fortitude, focus and at least the following key steps:

- Separate your business leadership responsibilities from your parental obligations. Think like someone who has just purchased your business and put the priorities and needs of the business above the needs of the members of the former owner's family.

- Incorporate the behavioral principles of successful family businesses into your business leadership practices.

- Your business is (1) *a Family Business With a Future,* (2) *Grim Reaper Bait,* or (3) *a Dead Business Walking* (chapter 4). Decide which is the case and implement corrective actions accordingly.

- Continuously strive to push the **Net Value of your Enterprise** curve skyward.
- Give leadership succession planning high priority over ownership succession and start now. Personally implement your leadership succession planning as you would any other critical element of your leadership responsibilities.
- Identify potential causes of leadership succession failures in your business and initiate suggested corrective solutions immediately.
- Require positive commitment, **lead-by-example behavior** and timely, high productivity from all family-member employees. Remove those who believe that mediocre behavior is acceptable.
- Successfully orient your children to the business facts of life and restrict entitlements that you or your family members take directly as employees of your business.
- Remember that the business is yours; it is not your children's business. Don't make false promises or make your children's participation obligatory by telling them that they will someday lead or own your business.

Encourage them to identify and seek their individual professional passions.

- Provide structure and opportunities for interested members of the next generation (children or others) to earn their way and put their skin in the game.
- Use clear, current job descriptions to facilitate all employment choices, job assignments, promotion decisions, compensation programs, and leadership selections.
- Starting with you, objectively identify and confirm the capabilities, qualifications, strengths, special talents, weaknesses, professional passions, and aspirations of all employees and employment candidates, especially family members. Use this information for all employment choices, job assignments, promotion decisions, compensation programs, and leadership selections.
- Match employment and leadership candidates to the jobs for which they are fully qualified and the most capable candidates.
- Before choosing a successor, consider and evaluate the best options from at least the following possibilities.

    (1) Direct descendants

    (2) Extended family members

(3) Experienced leadership professionals from within and outside your business

(4) Acquisition of or merger with a compatible business that has fully qualified leadership in place to take the combined business forward expeditiously and successfully to a higher level

(5) Sale of the business while it is at its peak value and using the proceeds to fund the family's future professional adventures

- Ensure that potential top leadership candidates are fully qualified and have at least the same level of future leadership capability and commitment that made your business successful in the first place.
- Ensure that you objectively select the most qualified and capable candidate for replacing you, before any inadvertent or planned leadership or ownership succession steps take place.
- Sharpen and practice using your delegation skills to enhance your leadership impact and streamline your leadership succession selection. Create time to

shift from tactical to strategic business priorities and personal rejuvenation opportunities.
- Foster inclusive communication and teamwork within the next generation that encourage and support the leadership succession plan.
- Create and nurture a positive, performance-oriented, challenging culture, with focus on the needs of the business, *not* on employee—especially family employee—entitlements.
- Create and implement compensation plans and incentive programs that (1) pay competitive wages, (2) incentivize commitment, motivation, leadership, performance, and retention, and (3) can succeed without the need for entitlements.
- Use proven incentives to assist you in motivating employees. Refrain from using annual bonuses or share of equity.
- Structure ownership succession that supports your leadership succession plan. Avoid the use of trust funds if at all possible.
- Measure progress and make refinements to continually enhance leadership and leadership succession before starting any ownership or control transition of any kind.

- Seek professional help from advisors who have the experience, qualifications and information you need. ***Sound leadership succession planning is critical— it is not the time for amateur-hour advice.***

As your leadership succession plan is implemented, the second-generation participants will realize whom the new leader(s) should be, and they will help you make the tough selection decisions; you are not alone.

Even that seemingly scary (and here, hypothetical) possibility that your oldest son will learn that his younger sister will be your replacement can be planned and implemented much more easily and successfully than you can imagine. If your succession plan is created and implemented well, your son will understand clearly why his sister is a better choice, and he will support her because it is the best choice to benefit him and his family. And, quite possibly, he will be thankful that he does not have to take the top leadership responsibility but will instead get opportunities to do what he loves while his sister has the more difficult responsibility of leading the business.

The recommendations offered here will help propel your family enterprise to new levels of financial success and future health through your generation and many future generations.

We wish you great success!

Our forthcoming book, *Family Business: Practical Ownership Succession Planning*, will discuss*:*

- ✓ Ownership succession: Why, What and When
- ✓ The benefits of practical ownership succession planning
- ✓ The key causes of ownership succession failures
- ✓ Practical ownership succession alternatives; pros and cons
- ✓ Using corporate structures for ownership succession
- ✓ Selecting and using trust fund structures wisely and sparingly.
- ✓ Generational challenges and how to overcome them
- ✓ Implementing practical ownership succession while prudently retaining control until you have a practical leadership plan in place.
- ✓ Selecting the best ownership succession plan for your business

www.ingramcontent.com/pod-product-compliance
Lightning Source LLC
Chambersburg PA
CBHW021957170526
45157CB00003B/1038